A Child's Book of Parables

by
Sister Mary Kathleen Glavich, S.N.D.

OPTIMUS MAGISTER BONUS LIBER

Loyola University Press
Chicago 60657

Nihil Obstat: Sister Donna Marie Brodesca, O.S.U., D.Min.
                 Censor Deputatus
Imprimatur: The Most Reverend Anthony M. Pilla, D.D., M.A.
                 Bishop of Cleveland
Given at Cleveland, Ohio, on 7 February 1994.

The Nihil Obstat and Imprimatur are official declarations that a book or pamphlet is free of doctrinal or moral error. No implication is contained therein that those who have granted the Nihil Obstat and Imprimatur agree with the contents, opinions, or statements expressed.

Glavich, Mary Kathleen.
    A child's book of parables/Mary Kathleen Glavich.
                p. cm.
    Contents: The lost sheep—The beautiful pearl—The runaway boy—The house built on rock—The seeds—The enemy who was kind—The rich man and the poor man—The servant with the hard heart—The ten brides maids—The man who didn't give up—The three servants—The little mustard seed.
    ISBN 0-8294-0801-0 $2.50
    1. Jesus Christ—Parables—Juvenile literature.   2. Bible stories, English—N.T. Gospels.
    [1. Jesus Christ—Parables.   2. Parables.   3. Bible stories—N.T.]   I. Title.
BT375.3.G53   1994   94-2383
226.8'09505—dc20   CIP
                                                                       AC

Illustrations and cover art by Lydia Halverson.

ISBN 0-8294-0801-0   01 00 99 98 97 96 95 94   5 4 3 2 1

Contents

The Lost Sheep 1

The Beautiful Pearl 4

The Runaway Boy 5

The House Built on Rock 10

The Seeds 12

The Enemy Who Was Kind 15

The Rich Man and the Poor Man 17

The Servant with the Hard Heart 19

The Ten Bridesmaids 21

The Man Who Didn't Give Up 25

The Three Servants 26

The Little Mustard Seed 28

The Lost Sheep

Based on Luke 15:3–7

A man had a hundred sheep. One day one sheep was missing. The man left the other ninety-nine sheep and went off to look for the lost sheep. He walked and walked, looking behind bushes and rocks.

Suddenly the man heard "Baa! Baa!" and saw his sheep. How happy the man was. He gently picked up the sheep and set it on his shoulders.

When the man got home with the sheep, he called his friends and neighbors together. He said, "Be happy with me because I have found my sheep that was lost."

A person who does bad things goes away from God. Jesus said that such a person is like a lost sheep. When that person is sorry and comes back to God, everyone in heaven is full of joy.

❖ Ask Jesus to help you stay near him.

3

The Beautiful Pearl

Based on Matthew 13:45–46

Once there was a man who bought and sold pearls. He was always looking for fine pearls.

One day someone showed him a beautiful pearl that cost a great deal. The man wanted that pearl very much. He sold everything he owned in order to have enough money for the pearl. Then he went and bought the beautiful pearl and was very, very happy.

Jesus said that the kingdom of heaven is like this pearl.

❖ Tell Jesus how much you would like to live with him in heaven.

4

The Runaway Boy

Based on Luke 15:11–32

A man had two sons. One day the younger boy said to his father, "Why should I wait until you die to have your money? Give me my share now." So the father gave all he owned to his two sons.

A few days later, the younger son left, taking his share with him. He went to a country far away. There he spent all his money in bad ways, trying to make himself happy.

That year the crops did not grow, and there was hardly any food in the country. The younger son, who had no money left, was very hungry. He got a job taking care of pigs. Still he was very hungry. He even wished that someone would give him some of the pigs' food, but no one did.

Then the boy thought, "My father's workers have plenty to eat, but I am dying of hunger. I'll go to my father and say I did wrong. I'll ask him to treat me as one of his workers from now on." So the boy started walking home.

7

When the boy was still far off, his father saw him coming. Filled with love, the father ran to meet his son. He hugged and kissed him.

The boy said, "Father, I don't deserve to be called your son."

But the loving father didn't let him finish. He called his servants and said, "Hurry. Bring the best robe and put it on him. Put a ring on his finger and shoes on his feet. Prepare the fat calf, and let's have a party. My son was lost and now is home."

And they celebrated.

❖ Thank Jesus for loving you as the father in the story loved his son.

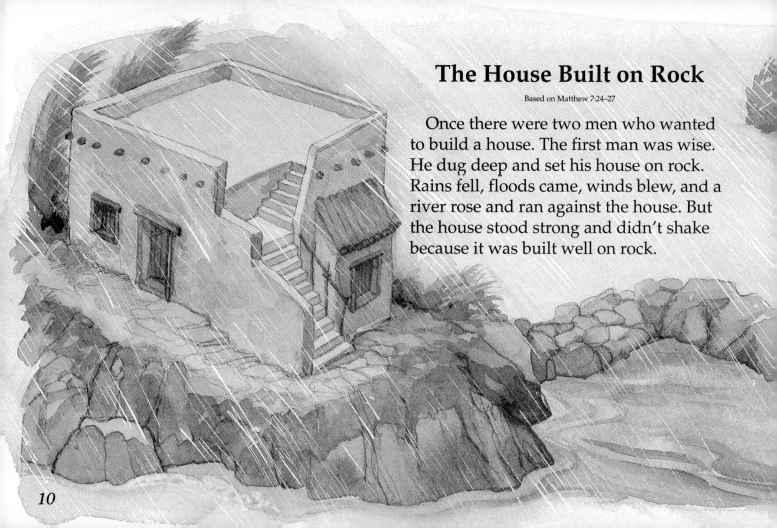

The House Built on Rock

Based on Matthew 7:24–27

Once there were two men who wanted to build a house. The first man was wise. He dug deep and set his house on rock. Rains fell, floods came, winds blew, and a river rose and ran against the house. But the house stood strong and didn't shake because it was built well on rock.

The second man was foolish. He built his house on sand instead of rock. When the rains fell and the floods came, and the wind and the river struck his house, the house fell and was smashed to bits.

Jesus said that a person who listens to him and does what he says is like the wise man who built his house on rock.

❖ Ask Jesus to help you listen to him and do what he says.

The Seeds

Based on Mark 4:1–9

A man went out to plant some seeds.
He scattered them on the ground.

Some seeds fell on a path, and birds
flew down and ate them.

12

Some seeds fell on rocky ground. They grew fast but had no roots. Under the hot sun they died.

Some seeds fell into thorns. The thorns grew and choked these seeds.

Some seeds fell on rich soil. These seeds grew tall and strong. The plants produced a large amount of fruit.

Jesus told us that the seeds on rich soil are like a person who hears his word and accepts it. That person does many good things.

❖ Tell Jesus you want his words to grow in your heart.

The Enemy Who Was Kind

Based on Luke 10:29–37

A man was traveling to Jericho. On the way robbers attacked him. They beat him and took his clothes. Then they left the man half dead at the side of the road.

A priest came down the same road. When he saw the hurt man, he passed right by on the other side of the road. A second leader of the people came to the spot where the man lay. When he saw the hurt man, he too passed by on the other side of the road. Then a Samaritan man came along. Samaritans were enemies of the hurt man's people. But the Samaritan felt sorry for the hurt man. He went over to the man lying by the road and bandaged his wounds. Then the Samaritan lifted the man onto his own animal and took him to an inn. There the Samaritan cared for the hurt man.

The next day the Samaritan gave the innkeeper two silver coins and said, "Take care of him. If you spend more than this, I'll pay you when I return." Which person was a real neighbor to the hurt man?

❖ Ask Jesus to make you kind to everyone.

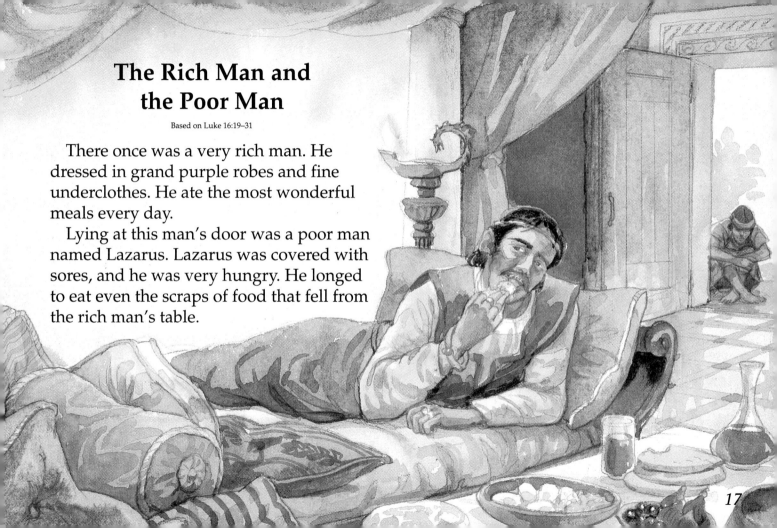

The Rich Man and the Poor Man

Based on Luke 16:19–31

There once was a very rich man. He dressed in grand purple robes and fine underclothes. He ate the most wonderful meals every day.

Lying at this man's door was a poor man named Lazarus. Lazarus was covered with sores, and he was very hungry. He longed to eat even the scraps of food that fell from the rich man's table.

17

When Lazarus died, angels took him to heaven. When the rich man died, he went to the fires of hell. The rich man could see Lazarus next to holy Abraham. The rich man called, "Abraham, send Lazarus to dip his finger in water and cool my tongue. I'm very hot and in pain from these flames."

Abraham answered, "Remember, you had good things on earth and Lazarus didn't. Now he is comforted while you suffer. Besides, no one is able to cross between heaven and hell."

Then the rich man begged, "Send Lazarus then to warn my five brothers to change their ways so they don't end up in hell like me."

But Abraham said, "They can listen to what God has taught them in the past."

The rich man argued, "If a dead man went to speak to them, I'm sure they would listen."

But Abraham said, "If they don't obey now, they won't listen even if someone comes back from the dead."

❖ Ask Jesus to give you a heart to share what you have with the poor.

The Servant with the Hard Heart

Based on Matthew 18:21–35

A king was collecting money that his servants owed him. One man owed a huge amount and couldn't pay it. The king ordered that the servant, his wife and children, and all that the servant owned should be sold. Then the man would be able to pay what he owed.

The servant fell to the floor and bowed to the king. He said, "Wait a while. I will pay back everything." The king felt so sorry for the man that he let him go. He said, "All right, you don't have to pay back anything."

19

Right after this, the servant met another servant who owed him a small amount of money. He grabbed the man and started choking him, saying, "Pay back what you owe me." The second servant fell to his knees and begged, "Give me time, and I will pay you back." But the first servant said, "No." He had the man put into jail until he paid back what he owed.

Others who saw what had happened told the king. The king sent for the first servant and said to him, "You wicked servant. I said you didn't have to pay back anything because you begged for mercy. Shouldn't you have treated your fellow servant the same way?"

Then the king sent the unkind servant to prison until he paid back all he owed.

❖ Ask Jesus to help you treat others as you want to be treated.

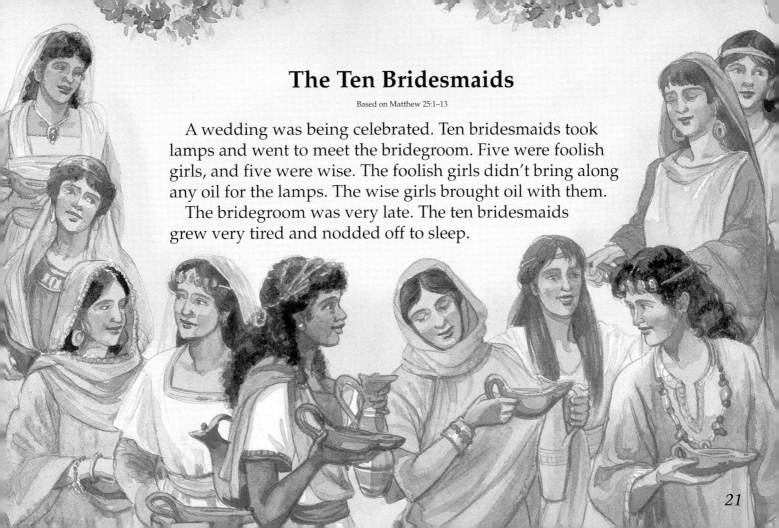

The Ten Bridesmaids

Based on Matthew 25:1–13

A wedding was being celebrated. Ten bridesmaids took lamps and went to meet the bridegroom. Five were foolish girls, and five were wise. The foolish girls didn't bring along any oil for the lamps. The wise girls brought oil with them.

The bridegroom was very late. The ten bridesmaids grew very tired and nodded off to sleep.

21

At midnight the cry came, "Look, the bridegroom! Come out to meet him!"

All the bridesmaids got up and got their lamps ready. The foolish ones said to the wise, "Give us some of your oil, for our lamps are going out." But the wise ones answered, "No, because there may not be enough for us and you. Go and buy some."

While the foolish girls went to buy oil, the bridegroom came. Those who were ready went into the wedding hall with him. The door was locked behind them. Later the five foolish bridesmaids came and called, "Lord, Lord, open the door for us!" But the bridegroom said, "I don't know you." The foolish girls were not able to go to the party.

❖ Ask Jesus to help you be good so that you are ready to go to heaven at any time.

23

24

The Man Who Didn't Give Up

Based on Luke 11:5–8

Late at night a man was surprised by a visitor. He had no food to give his guest. The man went to his neighbor and knocked on the door. He said, "Friend, lend me three loaves of bread. My friend who is on a journey has stopped at my house. I have nothing to give him to eat."

The man in the house said, "Don't bother me. The door is locked, and my children and I are in bed. I can't get up to give you anything."

The man at the door didn't give up. He kept knocking and asking. Finally, the man inside the house gave him bread.

❖ Pray to Jesus for something good for someone you know—and don't give up.

The Three Servants

Based on Matthew 25:14–30

A man was going away for
a long time. He called his
servants and gave them money
called talents to take care of. To
one servant he gave five talents,
to another servant two talents,
and to a third servant one talent.
As soon as the man left, the
servant with five talents used
them to make another five. The
servant who had received two
talents made two more. But the
servant who had been given one
talent dug a hole in the ground
and buried it.

When the man came back, the servant who now had ten talents said, "Master, I made five more talents." The master said, "Well done, my good servant. I will reward you."

The servant who had four talents said, "Master, I made two more." The master said, "Well done, my good servant. I will reward you."

Then the servant who had one talent said, "I was afraid, so I buried your talent. Here it is."

The master answered, "You wicked, lazy servant. Why didn't you put my money in the bank so it would earn more?" The master ordered, "Give this man's talent to the one with ten and throw this useless servant out."

❖ Ask Jesus to help you use the gifts he gave you.

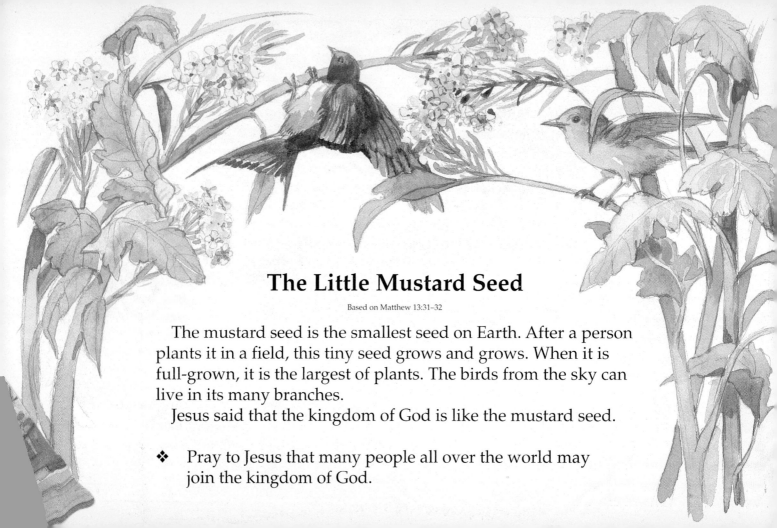

The Little Mustard Seed

Based on Matthew 13:31–32

The mustard seed is the smallest seed on Earth. After a person plants it in a field, this tiny seed grows and grows. When it is full-grown, it is the largest of plants. The birds from the sky can live in its many branches.

Jesus said that the kingdom of God is like the mustard seed.

❖ Pray to Jesus that many people all over the world may join the kingdom of God.